By
Richard Kent

Illustrated by Mike Dywelska

Hockey Talk
The question and answer book on the game of hockey.

Published by Funsport Publications Inc.

I.S.B.N. :0-9693804-1-0

Typesetting by Gandalf Typographers, Toronto
Printed by Maracle Press Limited

Printed in Canada

ACKNOWLEDGEMENT
Thank-you to James Duplacey and Joseph Romain at the
Hockey Hall of Fame, Richard Vroom at Miller Features,
Nancy Phillips, and the players from hockey and
baseball.

R.K./M.D.

To Ida Kent

According to legend the first hockey game was played on March 3, 1875. Apparently the game ended in a brawl. In what city did the game originate and in the beginning how many players per side took to the ice?

1

Montreal. Nine man teams played until 1886 when the rules were changed calling for seven man sides. In 1911 six man hockey came into effect.

Early hockey history, three part question. The gentleman pictured below donated a trophy in 1893 to be presented annually to ''the champion hockey club of the Dominion.'' Name the man, the trophy and the first winner of the trophy.

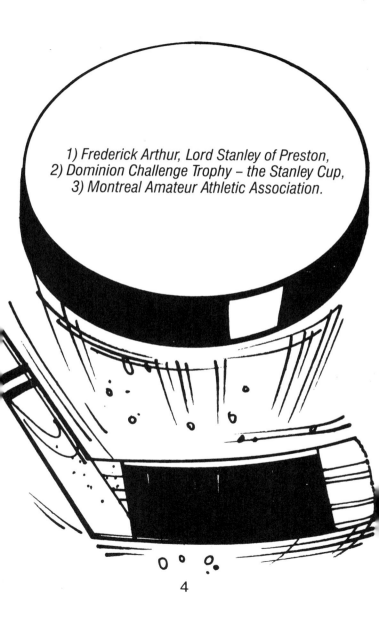

1) Frederick Arthur, Lord Stanley of Preston,
2) Dominion Challenge Trophy – the Stanley Cup,
3) Montreal Amateur Athletic Association.

Lord Stanley's Challenge Cup to the top team in the Dominion of Canada was soon heading to the United States. In 1917, the year before the National Hockey League was formed a club from the Pacific Coast Hockey Association became the first U.S. team to win the Stanley Cup.
Who took the Cup Stateside?

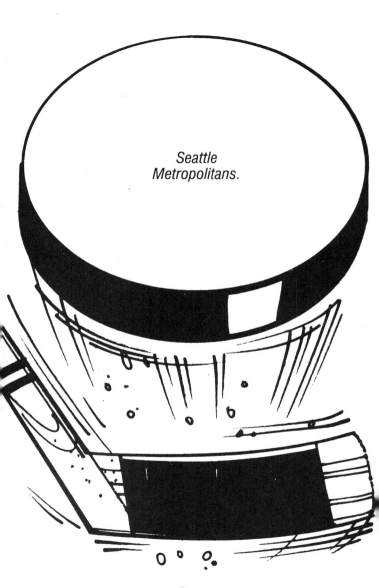

Seattle
Metropolitans.

Moving right along . . . During the 1988–89
National Hockey League season, including
playoffs, who were the busiest goalies,
appearing in the most games?

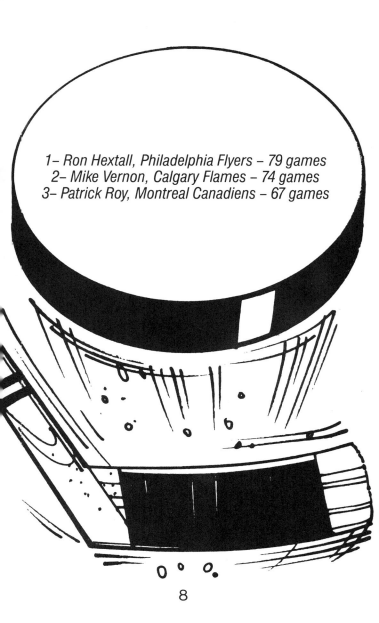

1– Ron Hextall, Philadelphia Flyers – 79 games
2– Mike Vernon, Calgary Flames – 74 games
3– Patrick Roy, Montreal Canadiens – 67 games

"Hello Canada, and hockey fans in the United States." "He shoots, he scores!" "Henderson has scored for Canada!" Foster Hewitt's memorable play by play brought the game alive for fans on many cold Saturday nights. Where and when did Foster do his first broadcast of a hockey game?

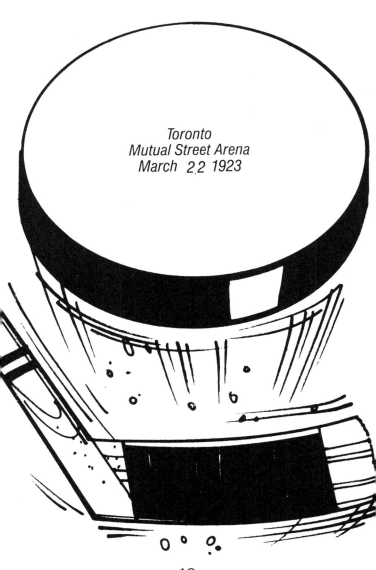

Toronto
Mutual Street Arena
March 22 1923

What National Hockey League franchises
did the following pioneer and build?
1) Charles Adams, 2) James Norris Sr.,
3) Conn Smythe, 4) Ed Snider.

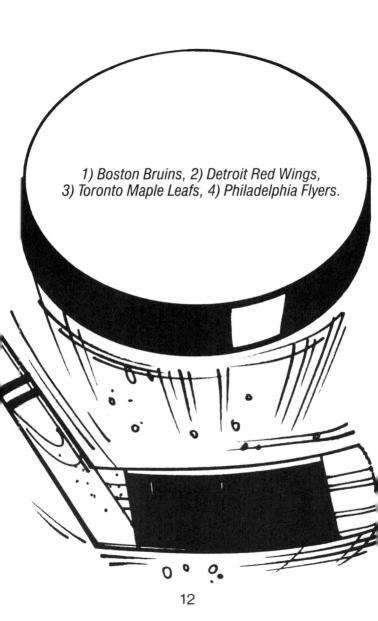

1) Boston Bruins, 2) Detroit Red Wings,
3) Toronto Maple Leafs, 4) Philadelphia Flyers.

Paul Henderson scores for Canada to defeat the Soviets in game eight of 1972 Canada-Russia series. Who scored the winning goal in games six and seven?

Paul Henderson scored the winning goal in games six, seven and eight.

14

Who was that masked man?
What NHL goalies wore the
following masks?

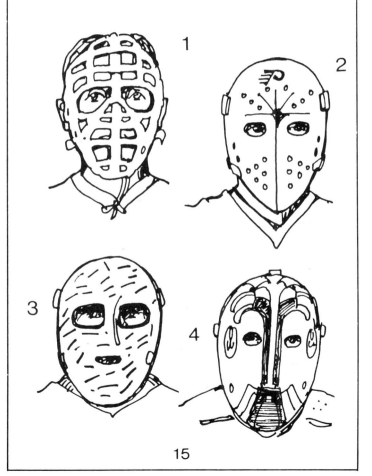

15

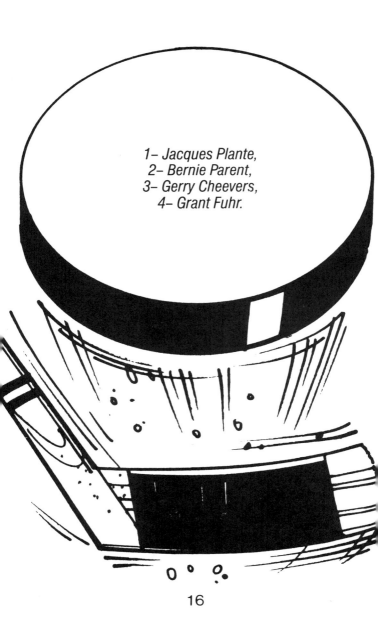

1– Jacques Plante,
2– Bernie Parent,
3– Gerry Cheevers,
4– Grant Fuhr.

16

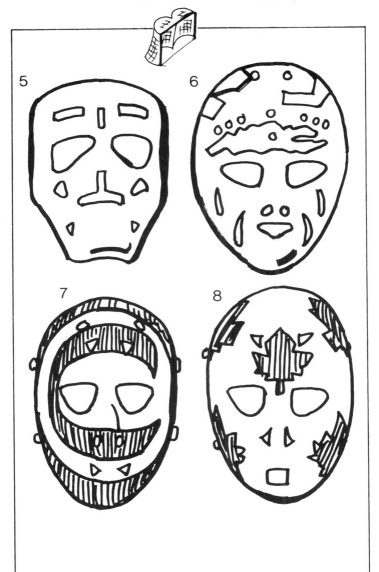

5

6

7

8

5– Terry Sawchuck
6– Glenn Resch
7– Ken Dryden
8– Mike Palmateer

18

On November 15, 1952 Hockey Night in Canada debuted on the CBC.

Who hosted that first show, who did the play-by-play and who was the sole sponsor of Hockey Night in Canada?

Host: Dave Price
Play-by-Play: Foster Hewitt
Sponsored by Imperial Oil.

20

The sharpshooters. Fifty goals in fifty games is one of the National Hockey League's greatest feats. Five gunners have shot fifty in fifty. Who?

Maurice Richard
Mike Bossy
Wayne Gretzky
Yari Kurri
Mario Lemieux

As of January 1, 1989, 40 men have served as President of the United States of America. As of that date four men have been President of the National Hockey League. Name the Presidents – of the NHL.

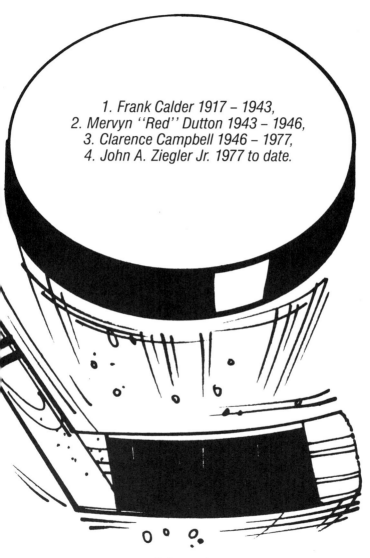

1. Frank Calder 1917 – 1943,
2. Mervyn ''Red'' Dutton 1943 – 1946,
3. Clarence Campbell 1946 – 1977,
4. John A. Ziegler Jr. 1977 to date.

Wild scramble in front of the net, defenseman and goalie both break their sticks. Other defenseman of defensive team grabs the loose puck and heads up the ice. Smooth skating defenseman gets to centre ice and rags the puck as his defense partner and goalie race to the bench and grab new sticks. Play immediately blown dead. What is the call?

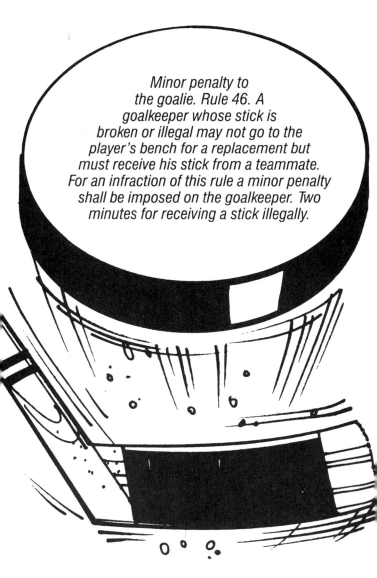

Minor penalty to the goalie. Rule 46. A goalkeeper whose stick is broken or illegal may not go to the player's bench for a replacement but must receive his stick from a teammate. For an infraction of this rule a minor penalty shall be imposed on the goalkeeper. Two minutes for receiving a stick illegally.

Two minutes for tripping, again. Perplexed
player discontentedly serves out another
minor to his dirty, dirty team, as a
polished powerplay peppers his short-
handed team's net. Finally short-handed
team gains possession of the puck and
fires it down the ice. Paranoid player,
fearing another infraction for doing
anything on the ice, climbs over penalty
box partition into his own bench.
Teammate jumps onto the ice making
team at full strength. Legal or illegal
substitution?

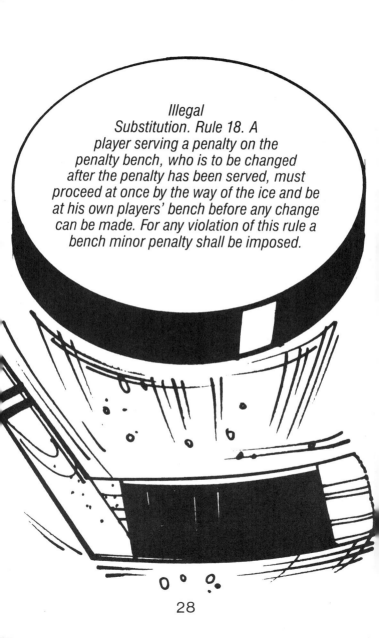

Illegal Substitution. Rule 18. A player serving a penalty on the penalty bench, who is to be changed after the penalty has been served, must proceed at once by the way of the ice and be at his own players' bench before any change can be made. For any violation of this rule a bench minor penalty shall be imposed.

The incomparable Gordie Howe played in over 2,400 professional hockey games scoring over 1,000 goals. In how many different decades did Gordie play pro and name the teams ''Mr. Hockey'' played for.

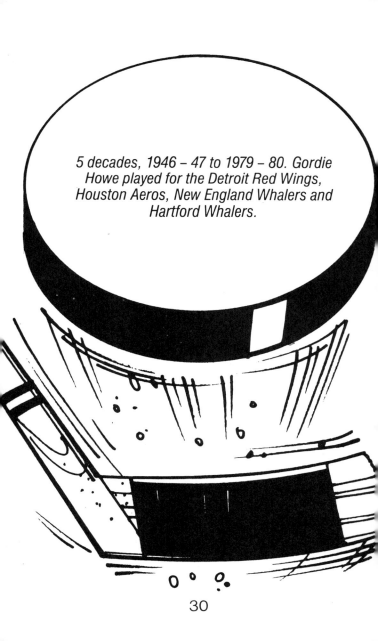

5 decades, 1946 – 47 to 1979 – 80. Gordie Howe played for the Detroit Red Wings, Houston Aeros, New England Whalers and Hartford Whalers.

From the pond to the pros, brothers dream of playing in the National Hockey League. These brothers made it: Odie and Sprague, Larry and Wayne, Peter and Frank, Dennis and Bobby. Surnames please.

Odie and
Sprague Cleghorn, Larry
and Wayne Hillman, Peter and
Frank Mahovlich, Dennis and Bobby
Hull.

Let's play Name the Defunct Franchise. These logos represented what teams during their stay in the NHL?

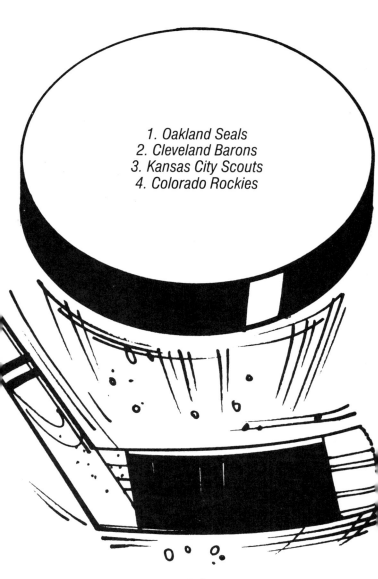

1. Oakland Seals
2. Cleveland Barons
3. Kansas City Scouts
4. Colorado Rockies

The following logos were worn by what
World Hockey Association teams?

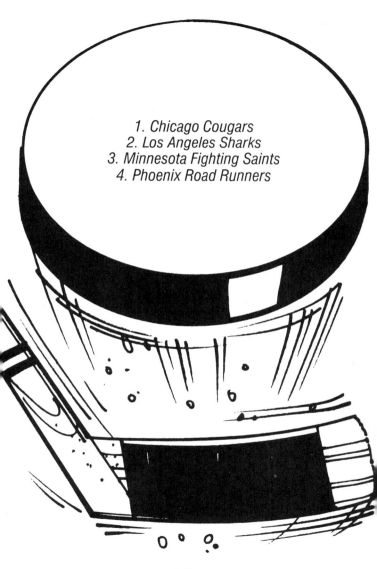

1. Chicago Cougars
2. Los Angeles Sharks
3. Minnesota Fighting Saints
4. Phoenix Road Runners

Glory days. During the 1960's the Toronto Maple Leafs won four Stanley Cups. During that decade outstanding Leafs won numerous individual awards. Name the three rookies who won the Calder Trophy, the two goaltenders who won the Vezina Trophy, the two fine gentlemen awarded the Lady Byng Trophy, and the outstanding play-off performer who took the Conn Smythe Trophy.

*Calder Trophy –
1961 Dave Keon, 1963
Kent Douglas, 1966 Brit Selby.
Vezina Trophy – 1961 Johnny Bower,
1965 Terry Sawchuk and Johnny Bower.
Lady Byng Trophy – 1961 Red Kelly, 1962
and 63 Dave Keon. Conn Smythe Trophy –
1967 Dave Keon.*

Name the nicknamed NHLer. The "Rocket" streaks down the right side and fires a pass over to the "Golden Jet" who is hammered by the "Hammer". Puck rolls into the "Snake" who deals off to the "Flower". "Flower" throws a nifty pass to the "Great One" who is immediately mauled by the "Mad Dog". Puck flips over the boards into the bench KOing "Toe" who bumps into "Gump". Who are these guys?

Maurice Richard,
Bobby Hull, Dave Schultz,
Jacques Plante, Guy Lafleur,
Wayne Gretzky, Bob Kelly,
Hector Blake, Lorne Worsley.

"Pie" hits the "Cowboy". "Ching" dings "King" on the wing. While "The Bomber" intercepts "Boom Boom", "Phantom Joe" disappears up the ice.
Real names please.

John McKenzie,
Bill Flett, Ivan Johnson,
Francis Clancy, Charlie Conacher,
Bernie Geoffrion, Joe Malone.

42

In 1962 – 63 Gordie Howe captured his
sixth and final regular season scoring
title. In 1980 – 81 Wayne Gretzky won his
first of seven consecutive scoring crowns.
In the years between Howe & Gretzky, 7
players were awarded the Art Ross Trophy
for greatest number of scoring points
during the regular season.
Name them.

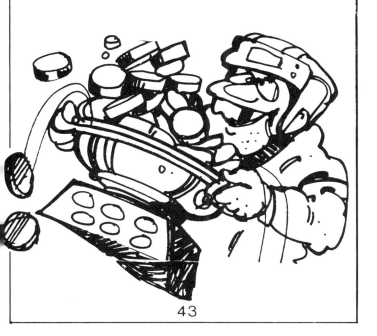

Stan Makita, 4 times
Bobby Hull, Phil Esposito, 5 times
Bobby Orr , 2 times Guy Lafleur, 3 times
Bryan Trottier and Marcel Dionne.

"If you can't beat 'em in the alley, you can't beat 'em on the ice." "I hated it in Pittsburgh, every time I did something wrong, they blamed it on me." "Put a fork in them . . . they're done." Those are three famous hockey lines from years gone by. Another three famous "lines" from the past were the Detroit Red Wings' Production Line, Buffalo Sabres' French Connection and the Edmonton Oilers' GMC line. Name the players who played on those great lines.

May 10, 1970. The Boston Bruins score in overtime to defeat the St. Louis Blues in four straight games to win the Stanley Cup. Name the goal scorer, goalie and defenseman involved in the historic goal.

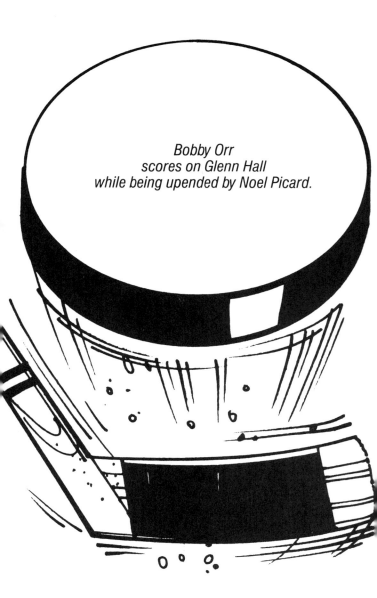

*Bobby Orr
scores on Glenn Hall
while being upended by Noel Picard.*

Double trouble. During the 1988–89
National Hockey League season, one
player wore 99, one wore 88, three
players used 77 and one skated with 66.
Who wore what?

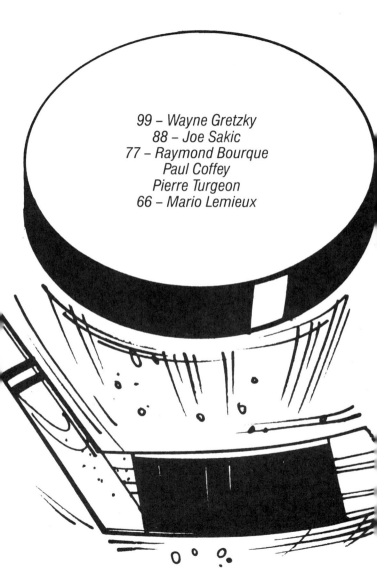

99 – Wayne Gretzky
88 – Joe Sakic
77 – Raymond Bourque
Paul Coffey
Pierre Turgeon
66 – Mario Lemieux

Zamboniology. A quick test of your basic Zamboni knowledge. Who invented the Zamboni, where was the first machine manufactured and in what decade was this powerful, practical ice resurfacer developed?

There have been many offensive defensemen over the years in the National Hockey League. Only six men though have scored 30 or more goals during the regular season. Name them.

Raymond Bourque,
Paul Coffey, Phil Housley,
Bobby Orr, Denis Potvin,
Doug Wilson.

''I am the
Hunter.'' During the 1988–89 season, four
Hunters played for a total of four different
NHL teams. These rugged individuals
stalked their opponents, racking up 953
penalty minutes. Name each Hunter and
his club.

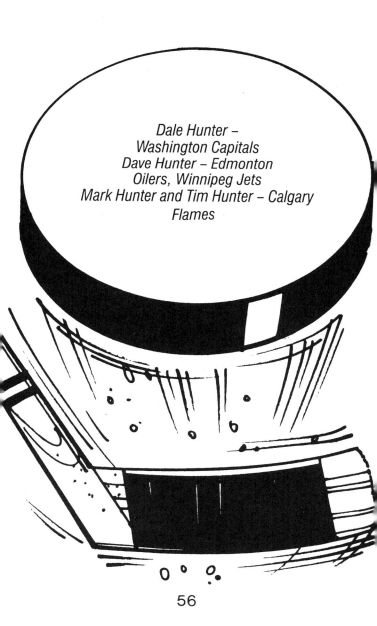

Dale Hunter –
Washington Capitals
Dave Hunter – Edmonton
Oilers, Winnipeg Jets
Mark Hunter and Tim Hunter – Calgary
Flames

Since 1985 four coaches have been awarded the Jack Adams trophy for excellence behind the bench. Three are still coaching in the National Hockey League, one stays upstairs. Name them.

1985 – Mike Keenan – Philadelphia
1986 – Glen Sather – Edmonton
1987, 1988 – Jacques Demers – Detroit
1989 – Pat Burns – Montreal

John Muckler
took over from Glen
Sather after the 1989 season.
Sather remains President and
General Manager of the Oilers.

Together these men played over 90 years
in the National Hockey League; they
competed in a combined total of over
6,500 regular season and playoff games.
Name the all-time leaders in games
played.

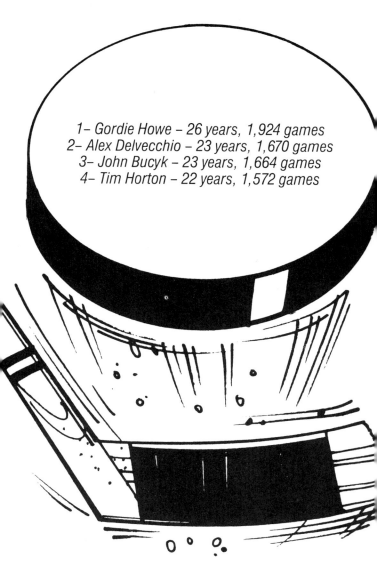

1– Gordie Howe – *26 years, 1,924 games*
2– Alex Delvecchio – *23 years, 1,670 games*
3– John Bucyk – *23 years, 1,664 games*
4– Tim Horton – *22 years, 1,572 games*

The following trophies are given by the
National Hockey League at the end of the
regular season. Two of the awards are for
individual achievement and one is
awarded for team excellence.
Name the trophies and the
achievement they represent.

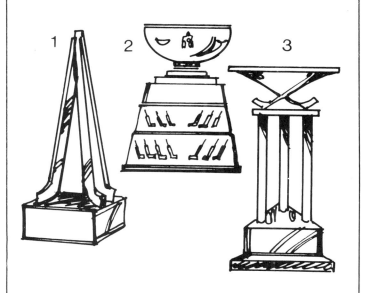

1   2   3

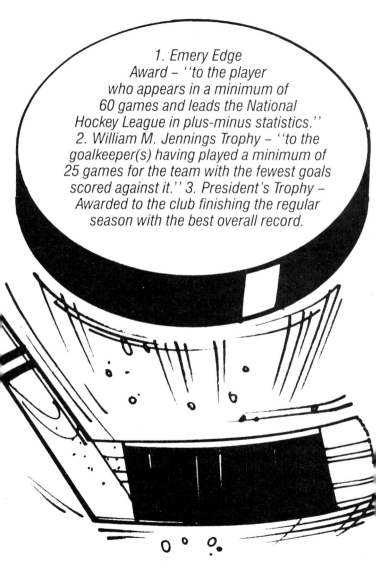

1. Emery Edge Award – ''to the player who appears in a minimum of 60 games and leads the National Hockey League in plus-minus statistics.'' 2. William M. Jennings Trophy – ''to the goalkeeper(s) having played a minimum of 25 games for the team with the fewest goals scored against it.'' 3. President's Trophy – Awarded to the club finishing the regular season with the best overall record.

Five Sutter brothers from Viking, Alberta played and coached on five different National Hockey League teams during the 1988-89 season. Name the five clubs that had Brent, Brian, Duane, Rich and Ron.

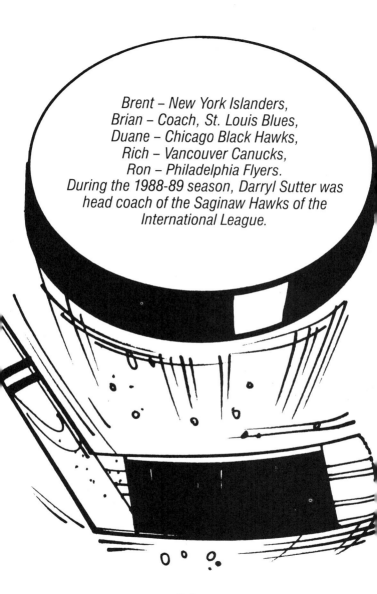

The good, the bad and the boring. Three
different NHL teams hold the record for
most wins, most losses and most ties
during the regular season.
Name the teams.

	GP	W.	L.	T.
_ _ _ _ _	80	60	8	12
_ _ _ _ _	76	17	35	24
_ _ _ _ _	80	8	67	5

	GF.	GA.	PTS.
_ _ _ _	387	171	132
_ _ _ _	197	225	58
_ _ _ _	181	446	21

Most wins –
1976-77 Montreal
Canadiens: 60. Most losses –
1974-1975 Washington Capitals: 67.
Most ties – 1969-1970 Philadelphia
Flyers: 24.

The World Hockey Association was in existence for seven years from 1972 to 79. The league championship trophy Avco Cup was won by four different franchises. Name them?

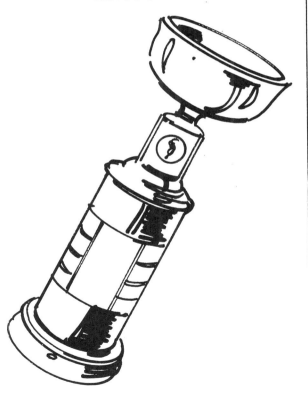

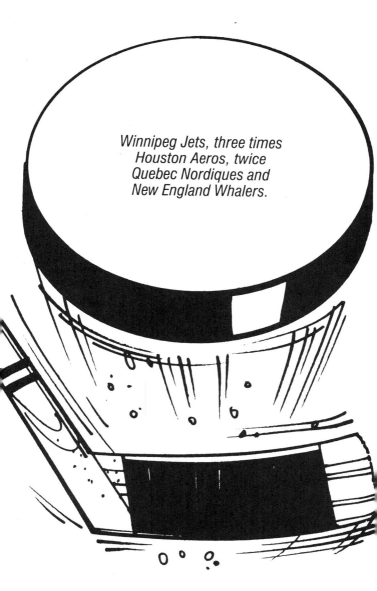

Winnipeg Jets, three times
Houston Aeros, twice
Quebec Nordiques and
New England Whalers.

Name the National Hockey League player with the most penalty minutes in a regular season and the NHLer with the most career penalty minutes?

Dave Schultz 472
minutes, Dave Williams
3,966 minutes.

70

"Slats" met "Rogie", "Trader Phil" battled "Tony O", and the "Cat" took on the "Senator". These former players, all now General Managers, had their teams meet in the first round of the 89 playoffs. Name the General Managers and their teams.

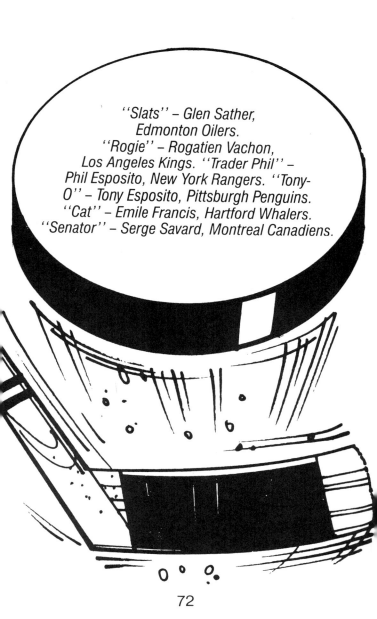

"Slats" – Glen Sather,
Edmonton Oilers.
"Rogie" – Rogatien Vachon,
Los Angeles Kings. "Trader Phil" –
Phil Esposito, New York Rangers. "Tony-
O" – Tony Esposito, Pittsburgh Penguins.
"Cat" – Emile Francis, Hartford Whalers.
"Senator" – Serge Savard, Montreal Canadiens.

In ten years of existence in the N.H.L.
the Edmonton Oilers own or share an
incredible ten playoff scoring records.
Two of these records were set playing the
Los Angeles Kings: the record for most
goals by one team in a game and the
record for most goals by both teams in
one playoff game. How many goals
were scored?

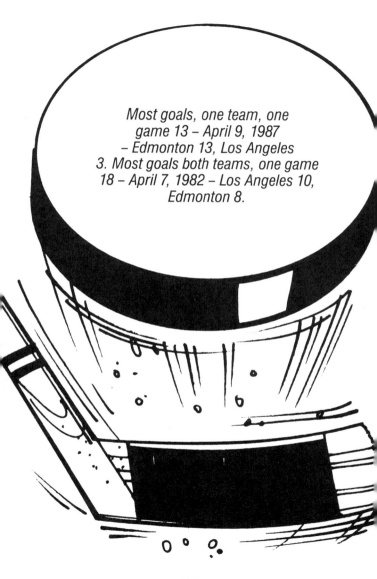

Most goals, one team, one game 13 – April 9, 1987 – Edmonton 13, Los Angeles 3. Most goals both teams, one game 18 – April 7, 1982 – Los Angeles 10, Edmonton 8.

Bobby Orr won the Norris trophy for top defenseman 8 times, Doug Harvey won the trophy 7 times. 6 other players have won the award more than once. Who?

Raymond Bourque 2
Paul Coffey 2   Rod Langway 2
Denis Potvin 3   Larry Robinson 2
Pierre Pilote 3

Wayne Gretzky owns or shares numerous National Hockey League scoring records. Here are a few great accomplishments the Great One hasn't accomplished. Name the players who hold the following records: most goals in one game: most points in one game: most points in one period: and the infamous most penalty minutes in one game.

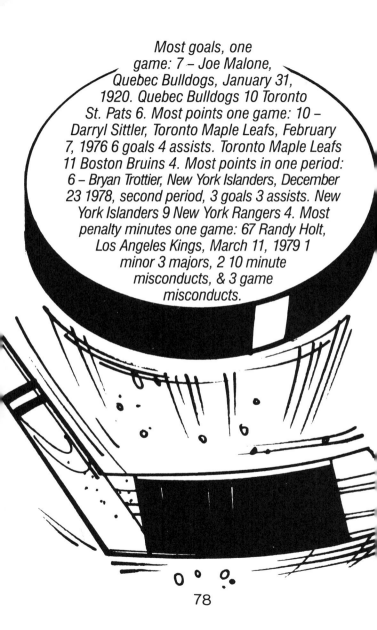

Most goals, one game: 7 – Joe Malone, Quebec Bulldogs, January 31, 1920. Quebec Bulldogs 10 Toronto St. Pats 6. Most points one game: 10 – Darryl Sittler, Toronto Maple Leafs, February 7, 1976 6 goals 4 assists. Toronto Maple Leafs 11 Boston Bruins 4. Most points in one period: 6 – Bryan Trottier, New York Islanders, December 23 1978, second period, 3 goals 3 assists. New York Islanders 9 New York Rangers 4. Most penalty minutes one game: 67 Randy Holt, Los Angeles Kings, March 11, 1979 1 minor 3 majors, 2 10 minute misconducts, & 3 game misconducts.

Four Swedish born players have
made the first or second National Hockey
League All-Star team. Who are they?

79

Hakan Loob
Pelle Lindbergh
Mats Naslund
Borje Salming.

It's 11 o'clock. Do you know where your hockey teams are?
In the National Hockey League three teams are planted in Gardens, two teams struggle in Forums, one plays in a Stadium and one rides under a Dome. Who plays where?

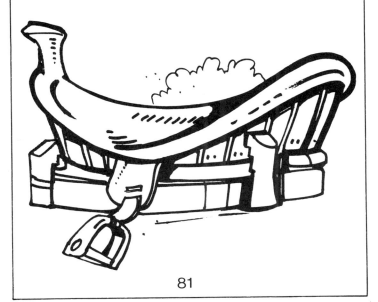

Boston Bruins-
Boston Garden, New
York Rangers – Madison
Square Garden, Toronto Maple Leafs –
Maple Leaf Gardens, Los Angeles Kings –
Great Western Forum, Montreal Canadiens –
Montreal Forum, Chicago Black Hawks –
Chicago Stadium, Calgary Flames – Olympic
Saddledome.

From the 1955-56 season to date, the Montreal Canadiens have won the Stanley Cup sixteen times. Five good men guided the Habs to these championships. Name the five men.

*Toe Blake,
Claude Ruel, Al MacNeil,
Scotty Bowman, Jean Perron.*

Four teams from that great hockey town Toronto have won Lord Stanley's Cup. The Maple Leafs were the last team to do so in 1966-67. Prior to the Maple Leafs what were the names of the three Toronto hockey clubs to win the Cup?

1921-22 Toronto St. Pats,
1917-18 Toronto Arenas,
1913-14 Toronto Blueshirts.

The three stars of the 1988-89 season are: Mario Lemieux, Wayne Gretzky and Steve Yzerman. No question there, the question is: name the last Juniour A club that each star starred for.

*Mario Lemieux –
Laval Voisins, Wayne
Gretzky – Sault Ste. Marie
Greyhounds, Steve Yzerman –
Peterborough Petes.*

Having one's number retired is a tribute
received by few men. The following teams
retired the following numbers.
Name the players honoured.
Edmonton Oilers 3   New York Rangers 7
St. Louis Blues 8   Boston Bruins 15

Al Hamilton
Rod Gilbert   Barclay Plager
Milt Schmidt

90

In 1980 the New York Islanders won their first of four consecutive Stanley Cups in dramatic fashion – in overtime. Who scored the winning goal? Name the team that was beaten and the goalie who was beaten?

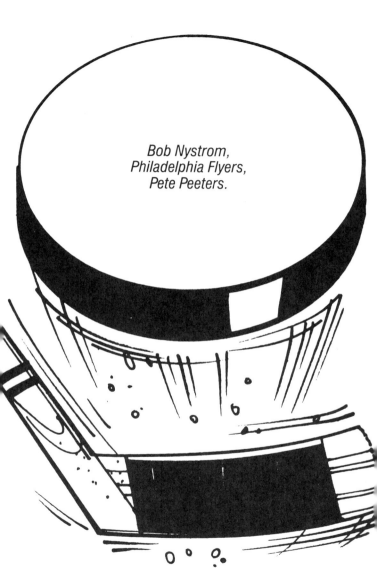

Bob Nystrom,
Philadelphia Flyers,
Pete Peeters.

Philadelphia Spectrum,
January 11, 1976. Philadelphia Flyers
versus the Central Red Army. Philadelphia
rough house tactics infuriate Russian
team. Finally, heavy hit flattens Russian
star and the Soviets leave the ice. Who
were the two coaches involved in the
game, who were the goalies, and who hit
whom to cause the game to be stopped?

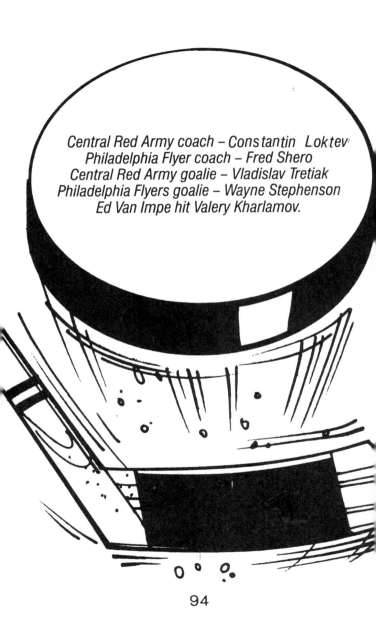

Central Red Army coach – Constantin Loktev
Philadelphia Flyer coach – Fred Shero
Central Red Army goalie – Vladislav Tretiak
Philadelphia Flyers goalie – Wayne Stephenson
Ed Van Impe hit Valery Kharlamov.

The battle of Alberta – the biggest and best rivalry in the National Hockey League. Win the province, go directly to the Cup. An Alberta team has been in the Stanley Cup final seven consecutive years, winning five times. Name the teams that faced-off in a final the last time the Oilers or Flames weren't there.

1981–82. The New York Islanders met the Vancouver Canucks; Islanders won the series in four straight games.

The Conn Smythe Trophy has been awarded since 1965 to the most valuable player in the playoffs; three players have won the award twice. Name them.

Bobby Orr,
Bernie Parent, Wayne Gretzky.

98

Name the four men who have competed in the most National Hockey League playoff games. Clue: naming three Canadiens and one Islander would be a good start.

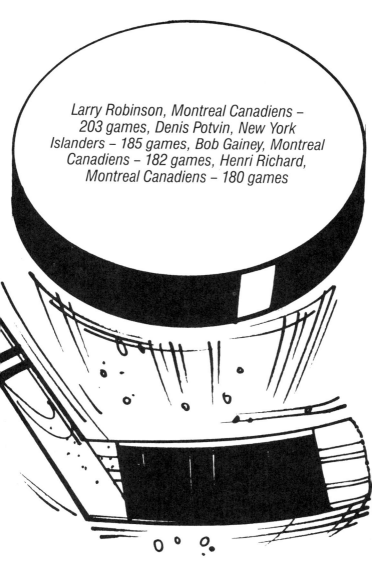

Larry Robinson, Montreal Canadiens – 203 games, Denis Potvin, New York Islanders – 185 games, Bob Gainey, Montreal Canadiens – 182 games, Henri Richard, Montreal Canadiens – 180 games

September 1976. Teams from Canada, Czechoslovakia, Finland, the Soviet Union, Sweden and the United States compete in the first Canada Cup. Fabulous hockey finished in fabulous fashion with an overtime goal winning the tournament. Who scored on whom, what teams won the gold, silver and bronze medals and who was the most valuable player of the tournament?

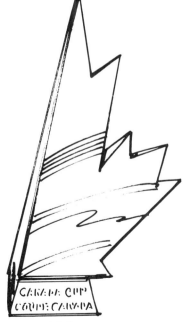

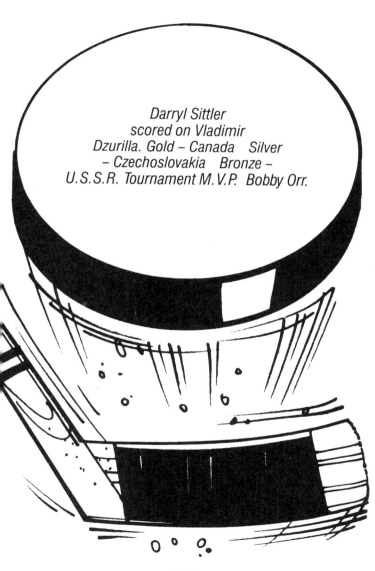

Darryl Sittler scored on Vladimir Dzurilla. Gold – Canada   Silver – Czechoslovakia   Bronze – U.S.S.R. Tournament M.V.P. Bobby Orr.

We are the champions. For the 1988-89 season, name the teams that captured 1) the Stanley Cup, 2) the Memorial Cup, 3) the Centennial Cup, 4) the University Cup.

1– Calgary Flames
2– Swift Current Broncos
3 – Thunder Bay Flyers
4– York Yeomen

104

All-time All-Stars. Name the goalie, two defensemen, centre, right and left wingers who have the most selections as first and second team All-Stars.

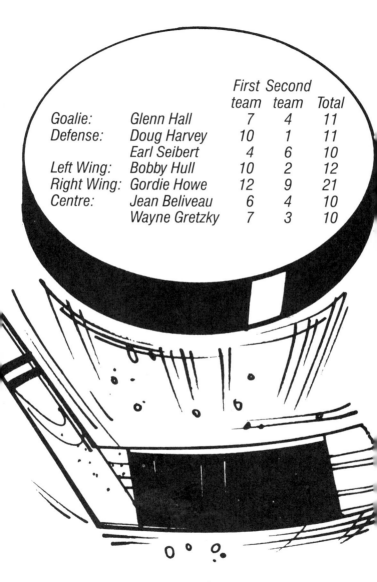

		First team	Second team	Total
Goalie:	Glenn Hall	7	4	11
Defense:	Doug Harvey	10	1	11
	Earl Seibert	4	6	10
Left Wing:	Bobby Hull	10	2	12
Right Wing:	Gordie Howe	12	9	21
Centre:	Jean Beliveau	6	4	10
	Wayne Gretzky	7	3	10

A lesson in logic: Sometimes making the playoffs in the National Hockey League is a dicey situation. After the 87–88 regular season, which teams went to the playoffs?

	Pts
New York Rangers	82
New Jersey Devils	82
Pittsburgh Penguins	81
Hartford Whalers	77
Quebec Nordiques	69
Los Angeles Kings	68
Vancouver Canucks	59
Toronto Maple Leafs	52
Minnesota North Stars	51

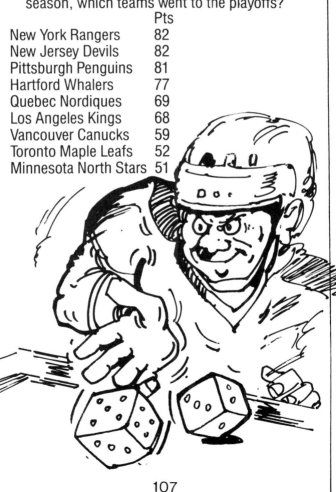

Toronto,
Los Angeles, Hartford,
New Jersey.

The Stanley Cup – the trophy symbolizing the World's Professional Hockey Championship. In 1989 the Calgary Flames became only the sixth team in the last twenty years to skate away with the handsome hardware. Name the five other teams who have captured the Cup since 1968 – 69.

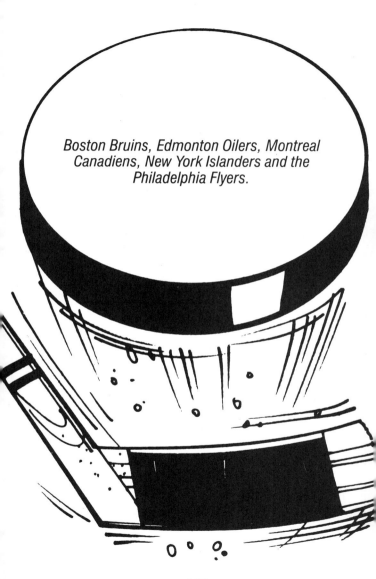

Boston Bruins, Edmonton Oilers, Montreal Canadiens, New York Islanders and the Philadelphia Flyers.

Talk Hockey
Send your Questions to
Funsport Publications Inc.
2032 Weston Road Box 114
Weston Ontario Canada
M9N 1X4

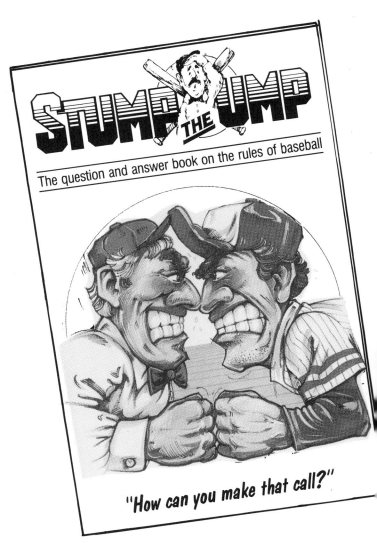